The Gargling Gorilla

and other stories

Roaring Good Reads will fire the imagination of all young readers – from short stories for children just starting to read on their own, to first chapter books and short novels for confident readers.

www.roaringgoodreads.co.uk

Other Roaring Good Reads from Collins

Spider McDrew *by Alan Durant*
Daisy May *by Jean Ure*
Witch-in-Training series by *Maeve Friel*
Mister Skip *by Michael Morpurgo*
The Witch's Tears *by Jenny Nimmo*

The Gargling Gorilla

and other stories

Margaret Mahy

illustrated by Tony Ross

An imprint of HarperCollinsPublishers

First published in Great Britain by CollinsChildren'sBooks in 2003
Collins is an imprint of HarperCollinsPublishers Ltd

77-85 Fulham Palace Road, Hammersmith, London W6 8JB

The HarperCollins website address is www.fireandwater.com

1 3 5 7 9 8 6 4 2

The individual stories *The Gargling Gorilla* and *The Runaway Reptiles* were
first published in Great Britain in the anthology
Bubble Trouble by Hamish Hamilton Ltd in 1991

Text copyright © Margaret Mahy 1991 and 2003
Illustrations by Tony Ross 1991 and 2003

ISBN 0 00 714840 2

Printed and bound in England by
Clays Ltd, St Ives plc

Contents

1. The Gargling Gorilla   7

2. The Dog-Magician   25

3. The Runaway Reptiles   59

The Gargling Gorilla

Rosa Sungrove, the well-known animal lover, was going out for the evening, so she needed someone brave and kind to feed all her pets. Tim, who lived next door, agreed to help her.

"Are you brave?" she asked him.

"Very brave," said Tim. "I'm not afraid of spiders or sharks or alligators. But I'm very kind, too."

"Good," said Rosa. "You sound just the one to look after my pets. Now, let me explain. The cat likes cat-snacks and the cat-snack pack is in the tall cupboard. The tall cupboard is beside the fridge, and the fridge is over there, on the other side of the sink. Right?"

"Right!" said Tim.

"However, when the vulture sees the cat being fed, he often gets a little peckish, and I don't want a peckish vulture around the place. The vulture-chunks are *inside* the fridge (over there on the other side of the sink). They are in the blue bowl. Right?"

"Right," said Tim, cheerfully.

The vulture looked down from its perch and clacked its beak. Tim smiled at it. He was not afraid of vultures.

"The wolfhound is outside under the camellia," Rosa went on. "When she smells the vulture-chunks, she gets very hungry. Her doggie-crunch is in the little cupboard *this* side of the sink, but her dish is on the bottom shelf of the tea-trolley beside the fridge over there on the *other* side of the sink. She *must* have her dish or she gets nasty. It's not her fault. She just does. Right?"

"Right!" Tim agreed.

"When the giant chinchilla rabbit hears
the rattle of the doggie-crunch being
poured into the dog bowl, it often thinks
it's hearing rabbit-nibble being poured
into the rabbit dish, and comes rushing
inside. Chinchilla rabbits are mostly
gentle, but this is a *giant* chinchilla
rabbit," Rosa warned Tim. "If you don't
feed her she will try to bounce on you,
and she is dangerously heavy. The rabbit

dish is the red one on the top shelf of the tea-trolley, there beside the fridge on the other side of the sink. And the actual rabbit-nibbles are in the large economy-sized purple packet on top of the fridge.

"And when you have finished feeding the animals you might like a little refreshment yourself. The tea is in the yellow jar at the end of the shelf on the other side of the sink. The bread tin is next to the yellow jar. The butter and cheese are in the fridge, and the biscuits are in the green box. Good luck! And now, I must go."

But at the door, Rosa stopped. "Oh, by the way," she called, "the gorilla is in the cupboard *under* the sink."

The gorilla! In the cupboard, under the sink!

Of course, most people know that gorillas are gentle and retiring, but Tim was unaware of this. The very bravest people can be scared of at least one thing, and Tim, though brave about absolutely everything else, happened to be scared of gorillas.

"When I took on this job," he thought to himself, "I did not know a gorilla was involved."

At that moment something in the cupboard under the sink began to gurgle, or perhaps to gargle. However, a gargling gorilla is just as scary as a gurgling one.

Tim made up his mind to keep away from the cupboard under the sink in case the gorilla put out a hairy hand and grabbed him as he was going by. But it wasn't easy, for the sink, and the cupboard under the sink, were in the very middle of the kitchen.

First, Tim fed the cat. He took the fire tongs and tied the tong handles to the handles of the broom and the mop. Then he reached over and, after several goes, opened the tall cupboard beside the fridge, sucking out the cat-snack pack with the vacuum cleaner.

Then, he lightly spiked the cat-snack pack with a fork tied to the handle of the thing you use to wash high-up windows, twisting it over so cleverly that the cat's dish was soon filled with delicious cat-snacks. The cat didn't seem to be at all frightened of the gorilla. It ate its dinner right in front of the cupboard under the sink.

When the vulture saw the cat was getting something, it stretched its neck greedily and flapped its wings. Tim did not want to walk past the cupboard under the sink in case the gorilla put out a hairy hand and grabbed an ankle. On the other hand, the poor vulture was certainly rather hungry. It began staring at the cat with a sinister expression. Being kind, Tim just *had* to feed it. First,

he used the tongs to reach past the sink to open the fridge. Then he took the thing you use to wash high-up windows (which still had the fork tied to the end of it) and he reached *into* the blue bowl inside the fridge. He spiked the vulture-chunks one by one, passing them (on the end of the fork) up to the vulture on its perch. The vulture gobbled them down, clacking its beak with happiness in between the gobbles.

The smell of the vulture-chunks brought the wolfhound in from the verandah. Her doggie-crunch was easy to reach, but when Tim tried to give it to her in a china soup tureen instead of her dish, she turned nasty and started snapping her teeth. She couldn't help it. Her dish was on the bottom shelf of the tea-trolley beside the fridge on the other side of the cupboard under the sink with the gorilla gurgling (or gargling) inside it.

The wolfhound saw Tim was hesitating. She put her giant paws on his shoulders and began slapping his face with a tongue like a wet carpet. It showed him just how sharp her teeth were: they were very sharp!

The tongs would not reach quite as far as the wolfhound's dish. Fortunately, a

fishing line that had belonged to Rosa's uncle was over the fireplace in the sitting room. Tim quickly cast the hook over the edge of the dish, reeled it in and filled it with doggie-crunch. Soon the whole kitchen rattled with the sound of the wolfhound crunching, the vulture clacking its beak, the cat snacking on cat-snacks and the gorilla gargling under the sink.

Tim was about to relax a little when the
giant chinchilla rabbit came bounding in.
It was a very big rabbit indeed. It made
nibbling noises and looked hungry. Tim
was so kind-hearted that he couldn't
stand it, and he wanted to help. But it
wasn't easy. He cast with his line again,
pulled the tea-trolley over, retrieved the

red rabbit dish, picked up the tongs and reached over and got the rabbit-nibbles down from the top of the fridge. Gargle-gargle went the gorilla under the sink, furious because Tim had been too clever for it.

When Rosa arrived home a moment later, she found the rabbit nibbling, the wolfhound crunching, the vulture clacking, the cat snacking and the disappointed gorilla gargling. The mop and the broom and the thing used for washing high-up windows were in their right places, the tongs were beside the fire and the fishing line was back over the mantelpiece.

"How well you've done!" she cried. "You are obviously brave *and* kind."

"The only one I haven't fed is the gorilla," said Tim, apologetically.

"The gorilla?" exclaimed Rosa.

"The gorilla in the cupboard under the sink," explained Tim.

"Oh!" said Rosa. She began to laugh. She opened the cupboard under the sink. "This is what I keep in the cupboard under the sink," she said. "The griller! It's for grilling cheese on toast. I just thought you might like some cheese on toast for your supper."

"But I heard it gargling," Tim said.

"Oh, those are just pipes leading to the sink," said Rosa. "They do gargle a bit."

The pipes gurgled as she spoke, and the back door opened.

"Do you mean there isn't a gorilla after all?" asked Tim. The back door shut.

"Oh, there is a gorilla," said Rosa, "but he's been away all evening. He is so shy and retiring, I encourage him to go to an evening class in flower arranging so he can get out and meet people."

As she spoke, the gorilla ambled in, bowed to Tim, and gave Rosa a beautifully arranged bowl of red and white roses.

Of course, Tim stayed for supper. Rosa made him a cup of tea, while the gorilla grilled toasted cheese sandwiches.

The cat snacked, the vulture clacked, the wolfhound crunched, the rabbit nibbled, the gorilla and Rosa and Tim gossiped, the pipes under the sink gargled (or gurgled) and the toasted cheese sandwiches sizzled happily in the griller.

The Dog-Magician

Slip Street was a short, shy street – the shyest street in the whole city. And it was not only timid but tidy, too. Up and down Slip Street the hedges were clipped, the gardens were weeded, the lawns were carefully mown and the doors and the gates were all painted a nice quiet green so that they would match the lawns. There was just one small exception.

At the very end of Slip Street was a battered old cottage. Grey paint peeled from its gate, and a notice on that gate said: For Sale.

"That cottage is just the right size for me and Merlin," thought Davy Shuttlewing. He patted his faithful dog. But then he hastily reached backwards to grab his faithful dog's faithful tail. "Don't wag!

Don't wag!" he hissed in a commanding whisper, looking left, then looking right. There was no one in sight. Davy sighed with relief... relaxed... cleared his throat and spoke softly. "We'll buy that cottage and once we're inside you can wag all you want to," he promised. "Unless we invite the neighbours in!" he added quickly. "No wagging if we're out in the street, and no wagging if we have a party! Got that? People won't want any wild parties in this street – just quiet get-togethers where they can smile at one another and talk in gentle voices about weather and income tax. No wagging!"

Davy had been living a roistering, rumbustical life for years and years, working as the top man in a team of

wandering acrobats and magicians. But he was sick of standing on the top of a human pyramid, pulling big, blue balloons out of his nose and whisking pink rabbits out of purple hats, while shouting, "Hey Presto!" at the audience. He was longing for peace and quiet at ground level, and that Slip Street cottage seemed as if it would suit him down to the ground. ("As long as Merlin doesn't wag his tail in public," he muttered, crossing his fingers.)

So, after a bit of wheeling and dealing, Davy moved into the cottage and began to do it up. His new Slip Street neighbours watched him shyly from behind their curtains. "It will be nice to have that

battered old cottage cleaned up," they muttered to themselves. But unfortunately on the very first day of his up-doing Davy made a serious mistake. He painted his gate which was fine, but he painted it *red*.

"A red gate! That's a show-off colour in a street like this!" the Slip Street people muttered behind their curtains. "We'll have to watch out for *him*."

Davy (leaning on his red gate) did his best to be friendly.

"Lovely day," he would say to passers-by, even if it was raining. But the Slip Street people gave uneasy smiles as they hurried on by without stopping to chat. And when Davy and Merlin walked down Slip Street together, although one or two people nodded to him across their neat hedges, no one ever asked him who he was or mentioned the weather. It is hard to invite people to a party when you don't know their names. As for the Slip

Street children – well, they had been told never to talk to strangers, which is good advice and none of them did.

"Perhaps they're anxious about dogs," Davy muttered, " even gentle dogs like Merlin. ("No! No! No!" he shouted quickly. "Don't wag your tail Merlin. Just smile and hang your tongue out. Don't you dare wag that tail of yours in this part of town.")

Davy had inherited Merlin from his Great Aunt Allywinkle who certainly wouldn't have fitted into Slip Street – not for a moment. Great Aunt Allywinkle would have painted *her* front gate purple, decorated it with shooting stars, and then danced on the gatepost, singing and waving her arms in the air. Until she had exploded (while trying to cast a complicated spell) she had been a wild wizard of a woman – and Merlin, her dog, had caught her magical powers as if they were measles. Not that you would notice this straight away. Merlin seemed to be one of those ordinary black and white dogs that you see around town, sniffing at telegraph poles and cocking a jaunty leg here and there. But Merlin was not an ordinary dog. He was a dog-magician.

This was a great problem for Davy. Of course, Merlin always wanted to wag his tail (as dogs do), but Merlin's wagging tail could be a wand as well as a tail, and sometimes when he wagged it (as dogs do) he wagged it in magic-mode. Then strange things happened. And not only that, being elderly, Merlin was just a little bit deaf. He wore a hearing aid which

Great Aunt Allywinkle had invented for him. All this made life complicated. Davy and Merlin would be strolling up Slip Street and see Mrs Happenstance tottering towards them in her brushed-up black boots. Davy would begin warning Merlin.

"Don't wag! Don't wag!" (After all, if Merlin wagged in magic-mode those black boots might turn into giant banana skins, or pink canoes, or steamed puddings covered in caramel custard.

(Davy didn't want a shy Slip Street neighbour to find herself ankle deep in custard and steamed pudding.) "Don't wag! Don't wag!" Davy would order Merlin.

Mrs Happenstance would look at him strangely as she tottered towards him, and Davy would hastily try to put things right.

"I was just telling my rascal of a dog to keep up with me," he would explain.

'Scalawag!' I was saying to him. 'Scalawag! Scalawag! Don't lag! Don't lag!'"

Mrs Happenstance would shrink shyly as she tottered by.

As for Merlin himself, though he loved getting out and about with Davy, he sometimes longed to get out and about on his own. He longed to sniff other people's gateposts and snuff the bags of rubbish, hidden neatly in garages and gardens. And at last, one Saturday morning when Davy (a man who was longing to give a party but was almost sure that nobody would come to it if he did) was sleeping, just a little sadly, until lunchtime, Merlin made up his mind to set out on his own. There was so much for a dog to see and do in the world beyond the red gate.

Of course, the red gate was neatly bolted, but Merlin wagged his tail at it. He wagged in magic-mode, and the bolt shot back obediently. Slowly, slowly, the red gate swung open and off went Merlin, out and away on his own, leaving Davy behind him – and not only Davy. Merlin had left his hearing-aid behind him, too.

It had rained during the night, and the Slip Street gutters were flowing like little

rivers. Sidney Silkweed (a small boy who lived between Mr Livermore's house and Dr Pincer's surgery) had been tempted to try paddling. Even though he was only four he already knew that public paddling would be frowned on in Slip Street, but he had hoped to make up for this by putting his shoes neatly side by side in a true Slip Street fashion. Once his shoes were settled he began to fold his socks which were new yellow ones. But, alas, he fumbled his folding and dropped his socks into the gutter. Immediately, the quick chuckling water seized them and swept them down a drain. The thought of walking barefoot back through Slip Street really frightened Sidney.

"I've lost my new socks! I've lost my new socks!" he was wailing softly to himself. Merlin stopped. He could see something was wrong, but, since he had left his hearing-aid at home he couldn't quite make out what Sidney was wailing.

"Lost a blue fox?" thought Merlin. "Poor boy! He's lost his blue fox and needs a new one. Well, I can arrange that."

Merlin wagged his tail twice. He wagged it in magic-mode. The water stopped flowing into the drain and began to bubble strangely. Then a large blue fox shot up through the bubbles and out of the drain. It began grinning and gambolling around Sidney, shaking itself dry. Sidney stared in amazement, then noticed it was wearing yellow socks on its pointed ears. The fox stood on its hind legs, sang two verses of the school song and then danced out into the road, something that

no blue fox should ever do. Mr Livermore, who was pedalling politely past on his push-bike, zig-zagged wildly, then ran slam bang into a telegraph pole. His bike fell sideways to the right of the pole while Mr Livermore toppled to the left, where he lay, tumbling and bumbling, at the edge of the road.

"Oh what a muddle! What a mad muddle!" he shouted in irritation.

"A puddle?" thought Merlin. "A glad puddle? He wants a glad puddle. Very strange! But, I can arrange that."

Merlin wagged his tail in magic-mode, and Mr Livermore found himself floundering in a deep, warm, brown puddle that had certainly not been there a moment earlier. Indeed, no one in Slip Street had ever seen a puddle like this one. It was so deep Mr Livermore felt he simply had to swim in it.

"A muddle! A muddle! I'm swimming in a puddle," shouted Mr Livermore.

"A fox! A fox! It's carried off my socks!" wailed Sidney, while the blue fox danced in front of him.

Old Mrs Happenstance came tapping along in her brushed-up black boots. Merlin smiled and waved his tongue at her, but she did not wave back. Her sharp gaze flitted from Sidney who suddenly seemed to be waltzing with the blue fox, to Mr Livermore bubbling in the big brown puddle. Then she looked at Mr Livermore's bicycle lying beside the telegraph pole, and shook her head.

"What a wham! What a bam! What a Slip Street slam!" she murmured.

Merlin listened, but, being a bit deaf, he didn't quite catch on to what she was murmuring.

"Lot of jam! Lot of jam! Lot of Slip Street jam," he thought. "Is that what she's wanting? Well, I can arrange that." And he wagged his clever tail in magic-mode.

Strawberry jam started to ooze out around the edge of the footpath. It swept in a little rosy wave towards Mrs Happenstance, and surged right across her brushed-up black boots before sweeping on past the Doctor's rooms towards the school end of Slip Street.

"Mercy me! I'm in a jam!" shouted Mrs Happenstance. "I really am! I really am!"

"A muddle! A muddle!" shouted Mr Livermore. "I'm troubling in a muddle... I mean I'm bubbling in a puddle."

Sidney and the blue fox slipped on the edge of the puddle and fell over sideways.

"I've boxed a fox!" wailed Sidney, "and I've lost my socks!"

They made such an unexpected racket that Doctor Pincer, a thermometer in one hand, came rushing out of his doctor's rooms.

"What's wrong? What's the matter? Have you got an ache?" he called as he came.

"A song? Some batter? Some cake?" thought Merlin, not quite catching on to what the doctor was really calling. "Well, I can arrange that!" And he wagged his tail in magic-mode.

Suddenly three strange people came running down Slip Street towards the little crowd by the puddle... two cooks and a waiter. One cook was carrying a huge plate of delicious cake: the other was holding a big bowl of batter. Close behind the cooks came the waiter, pushing a little barbecue with a frying

pan sizzling softly upon it. He had a pack
on his back filled with crusty bread sticks.
As they ran the cooks and the waiter
sang in perfect harmony:

"Feeling dismal dazed and lost?
You need a pancake lightly tossed.
Feeling life's a bad mistake?
Try a slice of sunshine cake!"

"Gracious me!" muttered the Doctor.
"This can't be Slip Street. What's

happening to me?" And he immediately put the thermometer into his mouth and began to take his own pulse. Meanwhile the first cook began passing slices of cake to Sidney, Mr Livermore and Mrs Happenstance, while the second cook, pouring the batter into the frying pan, began to make pancakes on the barbecue. The waiter broke up the breadsticks and began dipping them into the jam. Up and down Slip Street people came edging out from behind their green doors. There comes a time when even shy people just *have* to see what is going on.

"Have some cake!" the cake-cook shouted. "There's plenty for everybody."

"I'll be passing pancakes around in just a moment!" the other cook declared.

"Take cake in one hand and bread and

jam in the other," suggested the waiter running from gate to gate.

It was all so unexpected that people actually began to slide out into Slip Street, often forgetting to close their gates after them. Meanwhile the waiter was bending down to Mr Livermore, still floundering in that deep brown puddle.

"May I help you out of that mud puddle, Sir?" he asked. "It looks deep – very deep."

"It *is* deep! And it's warm! And it's

wonderful," shouted Mr Livermore with a beaming smile. "I was screaming, 'A muddle! A muddle!' and I accidentally swallowed a mouthful of mud."

"Oh sir, I am *so* sorry," said the waiter. "A piece of cake may take away that terrible taste."

"But the taste isn't terrible," cried Mr Livermore. "It's terrific. Because this isn't mud... it's chocolate. I'm swimming in puddle of warm chocolate. I haven't tasted chocolate for years and years. I've been too busy being shy to bother with chocolate. But now I remember just how wonderful chocolate can be. Oh, I love it. I *love* it. This isn't a bad puddle, it's a glad puddle and I'm happy to be chocolate-tasting in it."

"Chocolate?" shouted Sidney. He forgot about his socks and jumped into the puddle with Mr Livermore, leaving the blue fox to dance in circles with the yellow socks still on its ears. Seeing Sidney swimming in that puddle and lapping up chocolate as he swam, other children came running down Slip Street and jumped in, as well. Neighbours clustered around and began dipping fingers into the melted chocolate, then helping themselves to cake and pancake, accepting crusty breadsticks, rich with strawberry jam, all exclaiming and gossiping with one another.

The red gate at the far end of Slip Street burst open. Davy (still in his pyjamas) came running and racing towards the Slip Street party, waving his arms wildly.

"Merlin!" he shouted. "You've been wagging! Wagging in magic-mode! And you've forgotten to wear your hearing-aid."

Of course Merlin could not quite hear what Davy was saying.

"Lemonade!" thought Merlin. "Did he say something about lemonade? Yes, indeed! They'll need lemonade to wash down all that cake and chocolate. Well, I can arrange that." He wagged his wonderful tail.

"Don't wag your..." Davy cried desperately, but suddenly something leapt up under his feet and tossed him into the air. Davy was being lifted aloft by a jet of lemonade... a fantastic, fizzing fountain

filling the air with a sweet and lemony scent. He was tumbled over and over above Slip Street like a balloon-boy being tossed and tumbled by a small tornado.

At the sight of that lemonade-fountain some people ran back into their houses, leaving gates and doors open behind them.

"They don't want anything to do with me," thought Davy, tumbling around in the forceful flow of the lemonade fountain. "Not after Merlin's magic-mode tail-wagging!"

But a mere moment later, those same neighbours came running back again holding out mugs and cups and tumblers and champagne glasses.

"At last! At last! What a wonderful party!" they shouted to one another. "It's what we've always wanted, but we didn't know it until now. Thank you! Thank you," they shouted up to Davy, who, high above the footpath, was flipping and flopping in a fountain of fizz.

The party lasted all Saturday afternoon and on into the evening. The cooks took it in turns to toss the pancakes and to carry the cake around. There was always another pancake waiting to be eaten.

And the cake plate was never empty. Children swam up and down in melted chocolate, then danced under the lemonade fountain to wash away the chocolate they couldn't lick off themselves. Slip Street people started asking one another questions. ("Where did you get that lovely dress?" "Do you ever think of starting a Slip Street Cricket team?" "We won't need any dinner after this, but how about calling in for breakfast tomorrow?" "What is the meaning of life?" And so on.) Some of them began shouting up to Davy, telling him their secret thoughts even though he was flipping and flopping in his pyjamas and looking rather unreliable.

"...and congratulations on your dog. And on your red gate," Mrs Happenstance yelled. "This street has needed a dog and a red gate for a long time. Oh I do wish we all had dogs just like Merlin and I wish there were differently-coloured gates all the way up and down Slip Street."

Merlin, who was now wearing his hearing-aid, heard her quite clearly.

"Dogs like me for everybody? Differently coloured gates up and down Slip Street?" he thought. "What wonderful wishes. And I can arrange that."

He wagged his tail in magic-mode and, lo and behold... but by now you can probably work out just what happened next for yourself.

The Runaway Reptiles

Sir Hamish Hawthorn, the famous old explorer, was not happy.

"Oh, Marilyn," he cried to his favourite niece. "I long to go exploring up the Orinoco river once more, but who will look after my pets?"

"The Reverend Crabtree next door will feed the cats, I'm sure," said Marilyn. "He's a very kind-hearted man. And I will take care of the alligator for you."

"But, Marilyn," Sir Hamish said, "what about your neighbour? He might object to alligators."

Marilyn lived in Marigold Avenue – a most respectable street. The house next door was exactly the same as hers. It had the same green front door, the same garden and the same marigolds. A man called Archie Lightfoot lived there. He was rather handsome, but being handsome was not everything. Would he enjoy having a six-metre Orinoco alligator next door?

"Don't worry, Uncle dear," said Marilyn. "I shall work something out."

At that exact moment, by a curious coincidence, Archie Lightfoot was opening an important-looking letter.

Dear Mr Lightfoot, he read.

Your great-aunt – who died last week – has left you her stamp album, full of rare and valuable stamps.

"Terrific!" shouted Archie. Though he had never met his great-aunt, he had inherited her great love of stamps. Now, it seemed, he had inherited her stamp album as well. He read on eagerly.

There is one condition. You must give a good home to your aunt's six-metre Nile crocodile. If you refuse, you don't get the stamp collection. Those are the terms of the will.

"What will Marilyn Hawthorn say?" muttered Archie Lightfoot. "A beautiful girl like that will not want a six-metre Nile crocodile on the lawn next door. I will have to work something out."

That night, Marilyn Hawthorn tossed and turned. She could not sleep. In the end she decided to get up and make herself some toast. She could see the light next door shining on the marigolds. Archie Lightfoot was evidently having something to eat as well.

There is something about midnight meals that makes people have clever ideas. Sure enough, on the stroke of twelve, Marilyn Hawthorn suddenly thought of the answer to her problem.

The next day she ran up a large blue sun bonnet and a pretty shawl on her sewing machine, and borrowed the biggest motorized wheelchair she could find. Then she went round to her uncle's house.

Before leaving for the Orinoco, Uncle Hamish helped his niece settle the alligator comfortably in the wheelchair, packing it in with lots of wet cushions. The big sun bonnet nearly hid its snout, but Marilyn made it wear sunglasses to help the disguise.

"I shan't forget this," Sir Hamish said in a deeply grateful voice.

"Neither shall I," murmured Marilyn, wheeling the alligator out into the street.

As Marilyn pushed the disguised alligator through her front gate, she noticed Archie

Lightfoot pushing a large motorized wheelchair through his front gate, too. Sitting in it was someone muffled in a scarf, a floppy hat and sunglasses.

"My old grandfather is coming to live with me for a while," Archie said with a nervous laugh.

"How funny!" said Marilyn. "My old granny is coming to stay with *me*!"

The two old grandparents looked at

each other through their sunglasses and grinned toothily.

"Unfortunately," Archie added quickly, "my old grandfather can sometimes be very crabby. He has a big heart, but occasionally he works himself up into a bad temper. Do warn your grandmother not to talk to him."

"I have the same problem with Granny," Marilyn replied. "She is basically big-hearted, but at times she can be bad-tempered. If you try to talk to her when she's hungry, she just snaps your head off!"

At first, things went smoothly. Every day, Marilyn gave the alligator a large breakfast of fish and tomato sauce. Then she tucked the huge reptile into the wheelchair with blankets soaked in

home-made mud. Next, she wheeled it
into the garden and settled it down with
a bottle or cordial, an open tin of sardines
and the newspaper. The alligator always
looked eagerly over the fence to see
what was going on next door.

In his garden, Archie Lightfoot was
settling his old grandfather down with
tuna-fish sandwiches and a motoring
magazine. His grandfather blew a daring
kiss to Marilyn Hawthorn's grandmother.

Marilyn saw her alligator blow one back.

"You are not to blow kisses to a respectable old gentleman," she said sternly. The grandfather blew another kiss and the alligator did the same.

Marilyn smacked its paw. It tried to bite her, but she was much too quick for it.

While Marilyn Hawthorn and Archie Lightfoot were at work, the two old grandparents blew kisses to one another and tossed fishy snacks across the fence.

That evening, when Marilyn Hawthorn got home, she noticed that her alligator seemed rather ill. It sighed a great deal, and merely toyed with its sardines at supper. Marilyn felt its forehead. It was warm and feverish, a bad thing in alligators, which are, of course, cold-blooded. She took it to the vet at once.

"What on earth is this?" cried the vet, listening to the alligator's heart. "This alligator is in love!"

The alligator sighed so deeply it accidentally swallowed the vet's thermometer.

"It must be homesick for the Orinoco," Marilyn thought to herself. So she took a day off work, wrapped cool mud-packs around the alligator, and put it in the marigold garden – with a large photograph of the Orinoco river to look at.

As she was doing this, Archie Lightfoot's face appeared over the garden fence.

"Oh, I'm so worried about my grandfather," he cried. "I have had to take him to the vet – I mean, the doctor –

and he sighed so deeply that he swallowed a stethoscope."

"And I've had to take the day off work to look after my old granny," said Marilyn. "*She* has swallowed a thermometer."

"Ahem!" coughed Archie Lightfoot, clearing his throat nervously. "Perhaps,

since you are taking the day off work, you might like to slip over and see my stamp collection."

"I'd love to," replied Marilyn.

Marilyn Hawthorn and Archie Lightfoot spent rather a long time looking at the stamp collection. They forgot their responsibilities. But when they switched on the radio, they were alarmed to hear the following announcement:

"We interrupt this programme to bring you horrifying news. Two six-metre saurians – crocodiles, or perhaps they are alligators – both wearing sunglasses, are driving down the main road in motorized wheelchairs."

"Oh, no!" cried Archie Lightfoot.

"Oh, no!" cried Marilyn Hawthorn. Together, they ran outside. Their two lawns were quite empty.

"This is serious," gasped Marilyn. "Oh, Mr Lightfoot, I must confess that my grandmother is really an alligator."

"And my old grandfather's a crocodile," cried Archie. "I didn't dream that a lovely woman like you could be fond of reptiles."

"We can discuss that later,"said Marilyn, briskly. "First, we must get our dear pets back."

Quickly, they climbed into Marilyn's sports car and took off after the runaway reptiles. They soon saw them whizzing along in their wheelchairs. Overhead a police helicopter hovered, with several policemen and the vet inside it.

"It's very strange," said Marilyn, "but they seem to be heading for my uncle's house. I do wish Uncle Hamish was at

home. He would know what to do in a case like this."

The runaways turned into the street where Marilyn's uncle lived, but they did not turn in at his gate. Instead, they went through the next-door gateway, straight to the home of the Reverend Crabtree.

Imagine Marilyn's surprise when she saw her Uncle Hamish sitting on the verandah, showing the Reverend Crabtree his souvenirs of the Orinoco.

"Uncle, I didn't know you were back!"she exclaimed.

"Well, I have only just returned," he said, looking in amazement at the two reptiles. "The Orinoco wasn't as good as I remembered it, so I came home early. But Marilyn, why has my alligator split itself in two?"

"Oh, Uncle, this is not another alligator – it's a crocodile. And it belongs to Archie Lightfoot," Marilyn explained. "These two bad reptiles ran away together in their wheelchairs and came here."

By now the police helicopter had landed on the lawn, and the policemen, followed by the vet, came running over.

"Don't hurt those saurians," the vet was shouting. "They are not very well. They are in love!"

"Ah," said the Reverend Crabtree. "I understand! They have eloped and wish to get married."

The crocodile and the alligator swished their tails and snapped their jaws as one reptile, to show he was right.

"I'm not sure if I, a minister of the church, should marry an alligator and a crocodile," said the Reverend Crabtree doubtfully. "It doesn't seem very respectable."

"But it seems a pity to miss out on the chance of marrying two creatures so clearly in love," said Archie. Then, turning to Marilyn he added, "Suppose we get married, too. Will that make it more respectable? After all, we did bring these two reptiles together. It's only fair that they should do the same for us!"

So Marilyn Hawthorn married Archie

Lightfoot, and the crocodile and alligator were married too. Sir Hamish gave both brides away. Then he swapped over and became best man to the two bridegrooms.

Marilyn and Archie turned their two little houses into one large house, and their lawns into a swimming-pool for the two saurians. And they lived happily ever after, even though they had to begin every morning of their lives together feeding sardines to a handsome Nile crocodile and an Orinoco alligator – both with big hearts and even bigger appetites.

Mr Skip

★ MICHAEL MORPURGO

ILLUSTRATED BY GRIFF

When Jackie finds a broken garden gnome in a rubbish skip, she is determined to make him as good as new. In return, Mister Skip makes Jackie's wishes come true... almost! A fairy-tale for today from a master storyteller.

ISBN 0 00 713474 6

ROARING GOOD READS

Collins

An imprint of HarperCollins*Publishers*

www.roaringgoodreads.co.uk